ITALIAN MILITARY AVIATION

IN

WORLD WAR I 1914-18

Alexis Mehtidis

Published by
Tiger Lily publications LLC
For orbat.com

©ALEXIS MEHTIDIS

www.orbat.com

2005

ITALIAN MILITARY AVIATION IN WORLD WAR I 1914-1918

CONTENTS

- **1914** — 1
- **1915** — 3
- **1916** — 12
- **1917** — 21
- **1918** — 37
- **APPENDIX** — 55

1913 – 1914

In 1913 there were two Aviation Corps in the Italian Armed Forces, the Army's was composed of the 'Battaglione Aviatori' (Aviators Battalion, formed in June 1912) and the 'Battaglione Specialisti' (Specialists Battalion, formed in August 1910 and having, among others, one balloon park unit – reparto parchi aerostatici – with three specialists companies and one train company and the dirigibles unit – reparto dirigibili -) and the Naval Aviation.

The special ballooning section (sezione aerostatica speciale), among others, became organic to the newly-formed Artillery Specialists Group (Gruppo Specialisti di Artiglieria) on September 23rd, 1914.

Army Aviation, 1914

- Comando Battaglione Aviatori (Torino)

    - 1a Squadriglia Nieuport autonoma (Venaria Reale)

- I Gruppo (Aviano)

    - 2a Squadriglia Bleriot
    - 3a Squadriglia Bleriot
    - 13a Squadriglia Bleriot
    - 14a Squadriglia Bleriot

- II Gruppo (Pordenone)

    - 5a Squadriglia Nieuport
    - 6a Squadriglia Nieuport
    - 8a Squadriglia Nieuport

- III Gruppo (Padova)

    - 4a Squadriglia Bleriot
    - 7a Squadriglia Nieuport

- 1o Sottogruppo Biplani (S. Francesco al Campo)

    - 9a Squadriglia Farman
    - 10a Squadriglia Farman

- 2o Sottogruppo Biplani

    - 11a Squadriglia Farman (Brescia)
    - 12a Squadriglia Farman (Verona)
    - 16a Squadriglia Bleriot autonoma (Piacenza)

Naval aviation, August 1914

- M.2 airship ' Citta di Ferrara ' at Ferrara
- One V-type airship in trials at Vigna di Valle (it remained there until the spring of 1915)
- 14 sea-planes (Borel, Curtiss, Albatross, Farman-Guidoni) in the Naval School (Venice), the La Spezia Squadriglia and aboard various vessels. Later on in the year the La Spezia Squadriglia was disbanded and its sea-planes (the best of its 14 according to the official sources) moved to Venice, the rest was distributed in various coastal stations.

1915

Corpo Aeronautico Militare (Military Aviation Corps) was formed on January 7th, 1915 incorporating Aviators Flights Battalion (planes), the Specialists Battalion (airships among others) and the newly formed Battaglione Aerostieri (Balloonists Battalion, formed for free-flying and tethered balloons).

16a Squadriglia was disbanded in February 1915 and 15a Squadriglia was formed (equipped with monoplane Capronis).

Army Aviation, May 1915 (mobilisation)

Note: parentheses showing landing fields are those of mobilisation time.

- Comando del Battaglione Squadriglie Aviatori (Portoguaro)

- I Gruppo (also called gruppo squadriglie aviatori, at Portoguaro), assigned to 3rd Army (VII, X and XIV Corps) with the following squadriglie:

  - 1a Bleriot (Portoguaro)
  - 2a Bleriot (Portoguaro)
  - 3a Bleriot (Portoguaro)
  - 13a Bleriot (Torresella)
  - 14a Bleriot (Torresella)

- II Gruppo (Campoformido), assigned to 2nd Army (II, IV and XII Corps) with the following squadriglie:

  - 5a Nieuport (May 1915, not on mobilisation)
  - 6a Nieuport (not on May 1915, on mobilisation at Campoformido)
  - 7a Nieuport (Campoformido)
  - 8a Nieuport (Campoformido)

- III Gruppo (Pordeonone), assigned to Higher Command with the following squadriglie:

- 5a Nieuport (not on May 1915, on mobilisation at Campoformido)
- 7a Nieuport (on May 1915, not on mobilisation)
- 9a Farman (Pordeonone)
- 10a Farman (Pordeonone)
- 11a Farman (May 1915; getting new Farman Type 14 to replace Type 12s on mobilisation)
- 12a Farman (May 1915; getting new Farman Type 14 to replace Type 12s on mobilisation, on May 29th assigned to 2nd Army)
- 15a Caproni (on mobilisation at Piacenza)

- 4a Squadriglia Bleriot autonoma (on May 1915 at Padova; on mobilisation at Bazzera, Mestre for the defence of the Maritime Area of Venice)

Army Aviation (planes) comprised six Bleriot flights (37 planes and 30 pilots), four Nieuport monoplanes flights (27 planes and 20 pilots), four Farman flights (22 planes and 20 pilots) in total.

Battaglione Aerostieri:

- 6 field balloon sections (1a – 6a, sezione aerostaticha da campagna; horse-drawn)
- 2 fortress balloon sections (7a & 8a, sezione aerostaticha da fortezza; horse-drawn)
- 1 independent gas column (colonna autonoma gas) with an advanced balloon depot (magazzino aerostatico avanzato)

During 1915 Battaglione Aerostieri supplied trucks to its field sections making them
' autocarreggiate ' (self-carried), formed 9th fortress balloon section and I Fortress Balloon Sections Group (gruppo sezioni aerostatiche da fortezza)

By the declaration of war by Italy the Artillery Specialists Group (including artillery observation balloons) mobilised:

- 3 field balloon section on trucks (1a – 3a, sezione aerostatiche autocampale)
- 2 fortress balloon sections

- 1 balloon supplies section (sezione rifornimenti aerostatici)

During 1915 the Artillery Specialists Group disbanded its fortress balloon sections and formed the 4th Field Balloon Section on trucks.

Operational dirigibles were the following: P.5 (light, at Boscomantico), M.1 (heavy, at Campalto – Mestre -, later on given to the navy), M.3 & M.4 (heavy, in advanced stages of trials), one Parseval (reserve).

Naval Aviation on mobilisation

Naval Aviation had a few Borel, Albatross and Curtiss seaplanes distributed thus:

- Seven (various types) at Venezia (S. Andrea and Sabbioni)
- Four Borel at Porto Corsini
- Two Curtiss at Pesaro
- Two Curtiss at Brindisi
- Two Curtiss aboard R.N. Elba
- Fifteen Curtiss at the Scuola di Aviazione (Taranto)
- Dirigibles available were the following: M.2 ' Citta di Ferrara ' (heavy, at Jessi), V.1 ' Citta di Jesi ' (fast, at Ferrara) and V.2 (fast, being constructed), P.4 (light, at Campalto – Mestre -, ex-Army), one Forlanini F.3 being constructed.
- One embarked balloon section

June 1915

- Comando Squadriglie Aviatori (Pordenone)

- I Gruppo (Mortegliano):

  - 1a Bleriot (Chiasiellis)
  - 2a Bleriot (Chiasiellis)
  - 3a Bleriot (Chiasiellis)
  - 13a (Pozzuolo del Friuli)
  - 14a (Pozzuolo del Friuli)

- III Gruppo:

  - 5a (Campoformido)
  - 6a Nieuport (Campoformido)
  - 9a (Campoformido)
  - 10a (Campoformido)

During 1915, the Bleriot and Nieuport monoplane flights were disbanded, first 1a and 14a in June, then 2a Bleriot and 5a Nieuport in July.

1a and 2a Squadriglia Artiglieria (equipped with Caudron G.3 and Macchi Parasol respectively) were formed in 1915. These two flights constituted Gruppo Squadriglie Aviatori per l'Artiglieria.

In July a new 1a Squadriglia with Farman Type 1914 was formed. Another two flights were being formed with Voisin, having the numbers 16a and 17a for the time being, then being redesignated 5a and 7a. In the end of July one Sezione equipped with Caproni 300s (tri-motor bombers) was formed at Pordenone.

August 1915

- I Gruppo (Cervignano), assigned to the 3rd Army:

  - 11a MF 14
  - 5a Voisin

- II Gruppo (Udine), assigned to the 2nd Army:

  - 2a MF 14 (Campoforido)
  - 9a MF 14 (Campoforido)
  - 8a Nieuport (Clauriano), assigned to the 3rd Army

- III Gruppo (S. Maria la Longa), assigned to the 3rd Army:

  - 6a Nieuport (S. Maria la Longa)
  - 10a MF 14 (S. Maria la Longa)

- Gruppo Squadriglie Aviatori per l'Artiglieria (Medeuzza):

  - 1a Squadriglia Artiglieria (Medeuzza)
  - 2a Squadriglia Artiglieria (Medeuzza)

- Independent:

  - 12a Farman (Asiago), assigned to the 1st Army
  - 4a Bleriot (Bazzera)
  - Sezione Idrovolanti (Desenzano)
  - Sezione Caproni (Pordenone)

From August 27th, the confusion of flights numbering ended as Bleriot, Nieuport and Farman 1912 flight numbers were assigned to new Farman, Voisin and Aviatik flights.

September 1915

- I Gruppo:

  - 11a Farman
  - 5a Voisin
  - 7a Voisin

- II Gruppo:

  - 9a Farman

- III Gruppo:

  - 10a Farman

II Gruppo was disbanded and its single flight passed on to I Gruppo.

Other independent squadriglie.

14 squadriglie with 244 planes.

On November 1st, 1915 the Comando Battaglione Squadriglie Aviatori became Comando di Gruppo Squadriglie del Comando Supremo, with

Squadriglie Caproni 1a – 4a and the Sezione Aviatik da Difesa (formed in Aviano).

November 1st, 1915

- Comando Battaglione Squadriglie Aviatori (Pordenone):

    - 1a Caproni (Pordenone)
    - 2a Caproni (Pordenone)
    - 3a Caproni (Pordenone)
    - 4a Caproni (Pordenone)
    - Sezione Aviatik Difesa (Aviano)

- I Gruppo Squadriglie (S. Maria la Longa):

    - 5a Voisin (Chiasellis)
    - 7a Voisin (Chiasellis)
    - 10a Farman (S. M. la longa)
    - 11a Farman (Chiasellis)

- II Gruppo Squadriglie (Udine):

    - 6a Farman (Chiasellis)
    - 9a Farman (Campoformido)

- Gruppo Squadriglie Artiglieria (Medeuzza):

    - 1a Caudron (Oleis)
    - 2a Macchi Parasol (Medeuzza)
    - 3a Macchi Parasol (Medeuzza)
    - 4a Caudron (Gonars)
    - 5a Caudron (Oleis)

- Independent:

    - 2a Farman (Campoformido)
    - 8a Nieuport (Campoformido)
    - 1a Farman (Verona)
    - 12a Farman (Asiago)

- 3a Aviatik (Brescia)
- Sezione Idro (Desenzano)

From December 1st, 1915 the Squadriglie designation system existing (Squadriglie having the type of plane flown in their designations) was abolished in an attempt to rationalise it. Squadriglie became da Offesa (offensive, i.e. attack), da Ricognizione e Combattimento (reconnaissance and combat), da Artiglieria (artillery) and da Caccia (fighter). So:

8a Nieuport became 1a Squadriglia Caccia.
Aviano Sezione Aviatik became 4a Squadriglia Caccia.
3a Aviatik became 3a Squadriglia Caccia.
3a, 4a and 8a were left vacant for Ricognizione e Combattimento Squadriglie to be formed.

2a Farman and 1a Caccia formed Gruppo Squadriglie per la Difesa di Udine.
III Gruppo was reconstituted with 1a Ricognizione, 12a Ricognizione, 3a Caccia, 4a Caccia, 5a Offesa and Sezione Idro.

December 1915

- Comando Battaglione Squadriglie Aviatori (Pordenone):

    - 1a Sq. Offesa Caproni (Pordenone and Aviano)
    - 2a Sq. Offesa Caproni (Pordenone and Aviano)
    - 3a Sq. Offesa Caproni (Pordenone and Aviano)
    - 4a Sq. Offesa Caproni (Pordenone and Aviano)
    - 5a Sq. Offesa Caproni (Pordenone and Aviano)

- Comando I Gruppo (S. Maria La Longa), assigned to 3rd Army:

    - 5a Sq. Voisin (Chiasellis)
    - 7a Sq. Voisin (Chiasellis)
    - 10a Sq. Farman (S. Maria La Longa)
    - 11a Sq. Farman (Chiasellis)

- Comando II Gruppo (Udine), assigned to 2nd Army:

- 6a Sq. Farman (Chiasellis)
- 9a Sq. Farman (Campoformido)

- Comando III Gruppo (Verona), assigned to 1st Army:

  - 5a Sq. Offesa Caproni (Verona)
  - 1a Sq. Farman (Caproni)
  - 12a Sq. Farman (Asiago)
  - 3a Sq. Caccia Aviatik (Brescia)
  - 4a Sq. Caccia Aviatik (Verona)
  - Sezione Idrovolanti (Desenzano)

- Comando Gruppo Aviazione per Artiglieria:

  - 1a Sq. Caudron (Oleis), assigned to 1st Army
  - 5a Sq. Caudron (Oleis), assigned to 2nd Army
  - 2a Sq. Caudron (Risano-Chiasottis), assigned to 3rd Army
  - 3a Sq. Caudron (Gonars), assigned to 3rd Army
  - 4a Sq. Caudron (Gonars), assigned to 3rd Army

- Gruppo Squadriglie per Difesa antiaerea di Udine:

  - 2a Sq. Farman (Campoformido)
  - 1a Sq. Caccia Nieuport (Campoformido)

Naval aviation, end of 1915

- Two Lohner seaplanes at Grado
- Ten Albatros and other types at Venezia
- Nine planes at Porto Corsini
- Four Curtiss aboard R.N. ' Europa '
- Eighteen (Curtiss ?) at the Scuola di Volo at Taranto

Naval aviation was reinforced by ten seaplanes (and their personnel) from France, assigned to Venezia and Brindisi, and six Nieuport fighters of the French Army Aviation, destined for Venezia.

New acquisitions during the year were:

- One 15000 m^3 Forlanini-type airship

- 6 Albatross sea-planes (Enea Bossi-made)
- 24 Flying Boat-type sea-planes
- 18 Curtiss America sea-planes
- 10 Caproni Ca.3

Balloon units, 1915

Italy: 6 field balloon sections (1a – 6a), 3 artillery balloon sections on trucks (1a – 3a), I Fortress Balloon Group (Sezioni 7a & 9a) in Venice, 8th Fortress Balloon Section in Verona, 1st Artillery Fortress Balloon Section in Codroipo and 2nd Artillery Fortress Balloon Section in Latisana.

1916

Having undergone a major expansion in the very year of its formation, 1916 was to be another momentus year in the history of the Corpo Aeronautico Militare (Military Aviation Corps). At the beginning of the year, the force consisted of 5 gruppo and 3 independent squadriglie

Army Aviation, February 1916

- Gruppo Squadriglie at the disposition of Comando Supremo (Pordenone):

    - 1a Sq. da Offesa
    - 2a Sq. da Offesa
    - 3a Sq. da Offesa
    - 4a Sq. da Offesa
    - 6a Sq. da Offesa
    - 7a Sq. da Offesa

All the above Squadriglie were at the Aviano and Pordenone landing fields.

- I Gruppo Squadriglie (S. Maria la Longa):

    - 5a Sq. Ric. / Comb. (Voisin, at Chiasellis)
    - 7a Sq. Ric. / Comb. (Voisin, at S. Maria la Longa)
    - 10a Sq. Ric. / Comb. (Farman, at S. Maria la Longa)
    - 11a Sq. Ric. / Comb. (Farman, at Chiasellis)
    - 2a Sq. Caccia (Cascina Farello)

- II Gruppo Squadriglie (Udine):

    - 4a Sq. Ric. / Comb. (Farman, at Pordenone)
    - 6a Sq. Ric. / Comb. (Farman, at Chiasellis)
    - 9a Sq. Ric. / Comb. (Farman, at Campoformido)

- III Guppo Squadriglie (Verona):

    - 5a Sq. Offesa (Caproni, at Verona)
    - 1a Sq. Ric. / Comb. (Farman, at Verona)
    - 12a. Sq. Ric. / Comb. (Farman, at Villaverla)
    - 3a Sq. Caccia (Brescia)
    - 4a Sq. Caccia (Verona)
    - 1a Sq. Idro (Desenzano)

- Gruppo Aviazione per Artiglieria (Chiasottis):

    - 1a Sq. Artiglieria (Oleis)
    - 5a Sq. Artiglieria (Oleis)
    - 2a Sq. Artiglieria (Risano)
    - 3a Sq. Artiglieria (Gris – Gonars)
    - 5a Sq. Artiglieria (Gonars)

- Independent Squadriglie for air defence:

    - 1a Sq. Caccia (Campoformido)
    - 5a Sq. Caccia (Milano)
    - 2a Sq. Farman

Army Aviation, April 1st, 1916

- Gruppo Squadriglie for Comando Supremo (Pordenone):

    - 1a Sq. da Offesa (two Caproni 300, at Pordenone)
    - 2a Sq. da Offesa (three Caproni 300, at Pordenone)
    - 3a Sq. da Offesa (three Caproni 300, at Pordenone)
    - 4a Sq. da Offesa (two Caproni 300, at Pordenone)
    - 6a Sq. da Offesa (four Caproni 300, at Pordenone)
    - 7a Sq. da Offesa (three Caproni 300, at Aviano)

- I Gruppo Sq. (S. Maria la Longa), assigned to 3rd Army :

    - 5a Sq. Ric. / Comb. (five Voisin, at Chiasellis)
    - 7a Sq. Ric. / Comb. (eight Voisin, at S. Maria la Longa)
    - 10a Sq. Ric. / Comb. (seven Farman, at S. Maria la Longa)
    - 11a Sq. Ric. / Comb. (eight Farman, at Chiasellis)

- 2a Sq. Caccia (eight Nieuport, at Cascina Farello)

- II Gruppo Sq. (Udine), assigned to 2nd Army:

  - 4a Sq. Ric. / Comb. (eight Farman, at Tolmezzo)
  - 6a Sq. Ric. / Comb. (eight Farman, at Chiasellis)

- III Gruppo Sq. (at Verona), assigned to 1st Army:

  - 5a Sq. Offesa (five Caproni 300, at Verona)
  - 1a Sq. Ric. / Comb. (seven Farman, at Verona)
  - 12a Sq. Ric. / Comb. (five Farman, at Villaverla)
  - 3a Sq. Caccia (eight Aviatik, at Brescia)
  - 4a Sq. Caccia (eight Aviatik, at Verona)
  - 1a Sq. Idro (nine FBA, at Desenzano |

- Gruppo Aviazione per Artiglieria:

  - 5a Sq. Art. (nine Caudron, at Oleis, assigned to 2nd Army)
  - 7a Sq. Art. (eight Farman, at Oleis, assigned to 2nd Army)
  - 1a Sq. Art. (Caudron, at Risano, assigned to 3rd Army)
  - 2a Sq. Art. (ten Caudron, at Chiasottis, assigned to 3rd Army)
  - 3a Sq. Art. (nine Caudron, at Gonars, assigned to 3rd Army)
  - 4a Sq. Art. (nine Caudron, at Gonars, assigned to 3rd Army)
  - 6a Sq. Art. (Farman, at Verona, assigned to 1st Army)

- Independent Squadriglie and Sezioni:

  - 5a Sq. Caccia (twelve Aviatik, at Milano)
  - 13a Sq. Ric. / Comb. (Farman, at Valona, Albania)
  - 1a Sq. Caccia (eleven Nieuport, at Campoformido)
  - 2a Sq. Ric. / Comb. (nine Farman, at Campoformido)
  - Sezione Difesa (three Farman, at Aviano)
  - Sezione Difesa (four Farman, at Ancona)
  - Sezione Tripoli (five Farman, at Tripoli, Libya)
  - Sezione Bengasi (Farman, at Benghasi, Libya)

A radical change in the numbering of the Squadriglie was established on April 8th, 1916. Numbers from 1 to 24 were reserved for bombing

Squadriglie, 25 to 40 for reconnaissance, 41 to 69 for artillery and the ones 70 and over for fighter.

Offesa Squadriglie retained numbers 1a to 7a.

1a, 2a, 4a, 5a, 6a, 7a, 10a, 11a, 12a and 13a Squadriglie da Ricognizione e Combatimento became 31a, 33a, 29a, 25a, 30a, 26a, 28a, 29a, 32a and 34a respectively.

The seven Squadriglie Artiglieria (1a to 7a) equipped with Caudron G.3 or Farman became 41a to 47a respectively.

The five Squadriglie Caccia became 70a to 74a.

I Gruppo had 25a, 26a, 27a, 28a and 71a Squadriglie.
II Gruppo 29a and 30a.
III Gruppo 31a, 32a, 72a, 73a, 5a Caproni and 1a Idro.
Gruppo Comando 1a, 2a, 3a, 4a, 6a and 7a Caproni.
Gruppo Artiglieria 41a to 47a.

At the same time Gruppo numbering was stabilised, Gruppo Comando became Gruppo IV and Gruppo Aviazione per Artiglieria became V Gruppo.

Balloonists Battalion formed its 10th Field Balloon Section.

Naval Aviation, April 1916

On April 9th, 1916 the Inspectorate for Submarines and Aviation (Ispettorato dei sommergibili e dell'aviazione) was established by the Navy Chief-of-Staff office (Capo di Stato Maggiore della Marina).

Army Aviation, May 1st, 1916

Gruppo VI (Squadriglie 45a and 47a) and Gruppo VII (Squadriglie 46a and 48a) were formed on May 1st, 1916.

- I Gruppo (Chiasellis), assigned to 3rd Army:

    - 25a (Chiasellis)
    - 26a (S. Maria la Longa)
    - 27a (S. Maria la Longa)
    - 28a (Chiasellis)
    - 71a (Cascina Farello)

- II Gruppo (Udine), in Zona Carnia:

    - 29a (Tomezzo)
    - 30a (Chiasellis)
    - 35a (Chiasellis)

- III Gruppo (Verona), assigned to 1st Army:

    - 5a (Verona)
    - 31a (Verona)
    - 73a (Verona)
    - 32a (Thiene)
    - 72a (Brescia)
    - 1a Idro (Desenzano)

- IV Gruppo (Pordenone):

    - 1a (Pordenone)
    - 2a (Aviano)
    - 3a (Aviano)
    - 4a (Aviano)
    - 6a (Aviano)
    - 7a (Aviano)
    - 8a (Comina)

V Gruppo (Chiasottis):
    - 41a (Risano)
    - 42a (Risano)
    - 43a (Gris – Gonars)
    - 44a (Gonars)

- VI Gruppo (Oleis):

    - 45a (Oleis)
    - 47a (Oleis)

- VII Gruppo (Verona):

    - 46a (Verona)

- 48a (Belluno)

- Independent Squadriglie and Sezioni:

  - 70a (Campoformido) for the defence of Udine
  - 33a (Udine) for the defence of Udine
  - 34a (Valona, Albania)
  - 74a (Milano)
  - Sezione 37a (Brescia)

Artillery Specialists Group formed 4 field balloon sections on trucks (5a – 8a).

Army Aviation, September 1st, 1916

The mobilised aviation force comprised of 369 pilots (140 officers and 229 N.C.O.s and privates), 162 observers and 123 machine-gunners. Aircraft available in the war zone were: 43 Caproni, 121 Farman, 28 Voisin, 38 Caudron G.3 and 7 G.4 twin-engined, 63 Nieuport, 16 Aviatik, 12 FBA planes for a total of 328 aircraft in seven gruppi and 42 squadriglie with the following dispositions:

- I Gruppo (S. Maria la Longa), assigned to the 3rd Army:

  - 25a Voisin (9 planes, Chiasellis)
  - 26a Voisin (9 planes, S. Maria la Longa)
  - 28a Farman (7 planes, Chiasottis)
  - 36a Farman (8 planes, S. Maria la Longa)
  - 77a Nieuport (14 planes, Cascina Farello)

- II Gruppo (Udine), assigned to the 2nd Army:

  - 27a Farman (9 planes, Campoformido)
  - 29a Farman (9 planes, Cavazzo Carnico)
  - 30a Farman (9 planes, Chiasellis)
  - 35a Voisin (12 planes, Campoformido)
  - 76a Nieuport (14 planes, S. Maria la Longa)

- III Gruppo (Verona), for the 1st Army:

- 5a Caproni (4 planes, Verona)
- 9a Caproni (5 planes, Verona)
- 31a Farman (12 planes, Verona)
- 32a Farman (10 planes, Villaverla)
- 71a Nieuport (12 planes, Villaverla)
- 72a Aviatik (8 planes, Brescia)
- 73a Aviatik (1 plane, S. Anna di Alfaedo)
- 75a Nieuport (11 planes, Verona)

- IV Gruppo (Pordenone), for Comando Supremo:

  - 1a Caproni (4 planes, Comina)
  - 2a Caproni (4 planes, Aviano)
  - 3a Caproni (4 planes, Aviano)
  - 4a Caproni (4 planes, Aviano)
  - 6a Caproni (4 planes, Aviano)
  - 7a Caproni (4 planes, Aviano)
  - 8a Caproni (4 planes, Comina)
  - 10a Caproni (4 planes, Campoformido)

- V Gruppo (Chiasottis), assigned to the 3rd Army:

  - 42a Caudron (10 planes, Bolzano)
  - 43a Caudron (6 planes, Sammardenchia)
  - 44a Caudron (9 planes, Gonars)

- VI Gruppo (Oleis), assigned to the 2nd Army:

  - 41a Caudron (10 planes, Bolzano)
  - 45a Farman (9 planes, Oleis)
  - 47a Farman (8 planes, Oleis)

- VII Gruppo (Nove di Bassano), assigned to the 1st Army:

  - 46a Caudron (7 planes, Castenedolo)
  - 49a Farman (9 planes, Nove di Bassano)

- Independent Squadriglie:

- 33a Farman (8 planes, Campoformido)
- 70a Nieuport (15 planes, S. Caterina)
- 79a Nieuport (13 planes, Istrana)
- 48a Caudron (8 planes, S. Pietro in Campo)
- 37a Farman (6 planes, Bergamo)
- 74a Aviatik (20 planes, Milano)
- 11a Caproni (4 planes, Tahiraga, Albania)
- 34a Farman (8 planes, Valona, Albania)

The Army and Navy aviation services unified their technical, ' aerial means ' construction and personnel sectors by the 1213 Royal Decree on September 7th, 1916.

Anti-aircraft Defence Groups (Grupi di Difesa antiaerea) were formed on September 14th, 1916:

- 1o Settentrionale, with the Squadriglie and sezioni assigned to the area of IV, V and VIII territorial Army Corps
- 2o Meridionale, with units assigned to the area of VII, IX, X and XI Army Corps

Aerial defence flights (squadriglie da difesa aerea) were given a new numbering on September 23rd, 1916, starting from 101. So 38a, 39a and 40a Squadriglie being formed were, respectively, numbered 101a, 102a and 105a.

Army Aviation, October 1916

The Balloonists Battalion formed 1st Aerial Obstructions Special Section (sezione speciale ostruzioni aeree).

Army Aviation, November 1916

Comando del Battaglione Aviatori ceased to exist on November 16th, 1916 and its officials transferred to the new Aviation Services Office - Ufficio Servizi Aeronautici (U.S.A.) - by the Comando Supremo and the Aviation Command Flights Office - Ufficio Squadriglie del Comando d'Aeronautica (Aviatori) - in Torino.

Army Aviation, December 1916

Operational dirigibles: M.1 (at Campalto), M.3 ((Bosocomantico), M.9 (Casarsa), M.10 (Spilimbergo), F.3 (Ferrara, reserve), P.5 (Pilots' Scool, Ciampino).

The Balloonists Battalion formed the 11th Fortress Balloon Section.

Balloon units, 1916

- Italy: 6 balloon sections on trucks (1a – 6a), 7 artillery balloon sections ' self-carried ' (1a – 7a), I Fortress Balloon Group (Sezioni 7a, 9a & 11a) in Venice, 8th Fortress Balloon Section in Verona, 1st Aerial Obstruction Balloon Section in Venice.
- Albania: 10th Balloon Section ' self-carried '
    - Macedonia (Greece): 8th Artillery Balloon Section ' self-carried '

1917

Another significant expansion was undertaken in 1917. More gruppo were added, and some of the gruppo expanded to 8 or even 9 squadriglie. Territorial defense units were formed. Naval Aviation, authorized the previous year, began to expand. All this necessitated a new squadriglie numbering scheme.

Army Aviation, January 1st, 1917

- IV Gruppo, assigned to Comando Supremo (Pordeonone):

    - 1a Caproni (Comina)
    - 2a Caproni (Aviano)
    - 3a Caproni (Aviano)
    - 4a Caproni (Aviano)
    - 6a Caproni (Aviano)
    - 7a Caproni (Aviano)
    - 8a Caproni (Comina)
    - 10a Caproni (Campoformido)
    - 13a Caproni (Comina)

- III Gruppo / Aeronautica 1a Armata (Verona):

    - 1a Idro FBA (Desenzano)
    - 5a Caproni (Verona)
    - 9a Caproni (Verona)
    - 31a Farman (Verona)
    - 32a Farman (Villaverla)
    - 71a Nieuport (Villaverla)
    - 72a Aviatik (Brescia)
    - 73a Nieuport (Verona)
    - 75a Nieuport (Verona)

- VII Gruppo / Aeronautica 1a Armata (Nove di Bassano):

- 46a Farman (Castenedolo & Trizzino)
- 49a Caudron (Nove di Bassano)

-

II Gruppo / Aeronautica 2a Armata (Udine):

- 27a Farman (Campoformido)
- 29a Farman (Cavazzo Carnico)
- 30a Farman (Chiaseliis)
- 35a Voisin (Campoformido)
- 76a Nieuport (S. Maria la Longa)

- VI Gruppo / Aeronautica 2a Armata (Oleis):

- 41a Caudron (Oleis)
- 45a Farman (Oleis)

- I Gruppo / Aeronautica 3a Armata (S. Maria la Longa):
  - 25a Voisin (Pozzolo del Friuli)
  - 26a Voisin (S. Maria la Longa)
  - 28a Farman (Chiasellis)
  - 36a Farman (S. Maria la Longa)
  - 77a Nieuport (Cascina Farello)

- V Gruppo / Aeronautica 3a Armata (Chiasottis):

- 42a Caudron (Medeuzza)
- 43a Caudron (Bolzano)
- 44a Caudron (Gonars)

-

VIII Gruppo (Albania):

- 11a Caproni (Tayraga)
- 34a Farman (Valona)

- Sezione Nieuport Tahuraga

- Independent Squadriglie:

  - 2a Idro FBA (Grado)
  - 12a Caproni (Benghasi, Libya)
  - 33a Farman (Campoformido)
  - 37a Farman (P. S. Pietro)
  - 47a Farman (Thessaloniki, Greece)
  - 48a Caudron (Belluno)
  - 70a Nieuport (S. Caterina)
  - 74a Aviatik (Trenno)
  - 78a Nieuport (Istrana)

- Territorial Defence units:

  - 101a Farman (Bari)
  - 102a Farman (Ancona)
  - 103a Farman (Brindisi)
  - 104a Farman (Tripoli, Libya)
  - 105a Voisin (Firenze)
  - Sez. Difesa Foligno
  - Sez. Difesa Ravenna
  - Sez. Difesa Rimini
  - Sez. Difesa Comina
  - Sez. Difesa Beghasi (Libya)
  - Sez. Difesa Roma
  - Sez. Difesa Bergamo

- Centro Formazione Squadriglie di Ghedi

- Centro Formazione Squadriglie di Arcade

The new system for numbering Squadriglie for special services was (from January 19th, 1917): 100 to 199 for defence and colonies Squadriglie, 200 to 220 for attack (offesa) Squadriglie of the navy, 221 to 250 for fighter Squadriglie of the navy and 251 onwards for seaplane Squadriglie.

Naval Aviation, January 1st, 1917

- Stazione di Grado with 6 L.1
- Stazione di Venezia with 8 L.1, 3 L.2 and 9 FBA
- Stazione di Varano with 5 L.1 and 2 FBA
- Stazione di Brindisi with 4 L.1, 6 L.2 and 9 FBA
- R.N. Europa with 6 L.1 and 1 L.2

Naval Aviation, February 1917

An Inspectorate for National (Sea) Traffic (Ispettorato Difesa del Traffico Nazionale) was established on February 17th, 1917 to address the problem of German submarines in the Mediterranean. It comprised of coastal artillery batteries, observation posts, escort vessels and of a series of seaplane stations all along the Italian coast.

Army Aviation, March 1917

All units of the balloon service were incorporated in the Military Aviation Corps and some of the existing numbers of its units changed. Its units were:

4 balloon sections groups ' self carried ' (I – IV, the last one was formed in March with Sezioni 17a & 18a)
1 fortress balloon sections group (V)
16 balloon sections ' self-carried ' (1a – 16a; 1a – 8a Artillery, 9a – 15a the ones mobilised by the Balloonists Battalion, 16a was the former 8th Fortress)
3 fortress balloon sections (25a – 27a, being the former 7a, 9a & 11a)

Army Aviation, April 1917

From April 5th, 1917 a new Order for Aviation in war was issued. According to it Balloon Sections (Sezioni Aerostatiche) were also assigned to the 2nd and 3rd Armies' Comandi Aeronautici, in addition to the air units already assigned. II and VI Gruppo (a total of nine Squadriglie) were additionally assigned to the 2nd Army Comando Aeronautica and I and V Gruppo to 3rd Army Comando Aeronautica. III Gruppo formed IX Gruppo with Squadriglie 37a (Bergamo defence), 72a, 73a, 74a (Milano defence), 75a and 112a (newly formed). IV

Gruppo Caproni (assigned to Comando Supremo) formed XI Gruppo with Squadriglie 3a, 4a, 6a, 7a and the newly formed 14a and 15a. X Gruppo was formed too and it was also assigned to Comando Supremo with Squadriglie 33a, 70a, 78a, 79a and 82a.

Army Aviation, May 1917

A new Aviation Order for the war zone came into being on May 2nd, 1917, forming (on May 10th) Comandi Aeronautici of the 4th and 6th Armies and the new XII Gruppo.

III Gruppo (to which 46a Squadriglia Ricognizione and the new 50a were assigned) exchanged its 71a with the 72a of IX Gruppo and it was assigned to the 1st Army. IX Gruppo had Squadriglie 37a, 71a, 73a, 74a, 75a and 112a.

The newly-formed XII Gruppo (48a, one section / 113a, one section / 83a Nieuport and the 35a that was newly-formed) was assigned to the 4th Army.

VII Gruppo (reformed on May 10th, with 32a, 49a and 79a) was assigned to the 6th Army.

Comando Squadriglie per Artiglieria was abolished and Squadriglie of its V, VI and VII Gruppi lost the ' Squadriglie di artiglieria ' naming.

- Aeronautica del Comando Supremo:

    - IV Gruppo (Squadriglie 1a, 8a, 10a, 13a and 14a)
    - X Gruppo (Squadriglie 33a, 70a, 78a, 79a and 91a)
    - XI Gruppo (Squadriglie 2a, 3a, 4a, 6a, 7a and 15a)

- Comando d'Aeronautica 1a Armata:

    - III Gruppo (Squadriglie 5a, 9a, 31a, 46a, 72a and 1a Idro)
    - IX Gruppo (Squadriglie 37a, 71a, 73a, 74a and 75a)

- Comando d'Aeronautica 2a Armata:

    - II Gruppo (Squadriglie 21a, 22a, 27a, 30a, 40a, 41a, 76a and 81a)
    - VI Gruppo (Squadriglie 24a, 29a, 45a and Sez. 113a)

- Comando d'Aeronautica 3a Armata:

- I Gruppo (Squadriglie 23a, 25a, 36a, 77a, 80a and 2a Idro)
- V Gruppo (Squadriglie 38a, 39a, 43a and 44a)

- Comando d'Aeronautica 4a Armata:

  - VII Gruppo (Squadriglie 32a, 49a and 79a)

- Comando d'Aeronautica 6a Armata:

  - XII Gruppo (Squadriglie 48a, Sez. 113a and Sez. Caccia)

- VIII Gruppo (Squadriglie 11a, 34a and Sez. 85a) in Albania

- Squadriglie 47a and Sez. 83a in Macedonia, Greece

- Squadriglie 12a, 104a, Sez. Tripoli and Sez. Tobruk in Libya

- 101a, 102a, 103a and 105a Squadriglie da Difesa and fourteen Sezioni da Difesa

Naval Aviation, June 1917

I Navy Balloon Section (sezione aerostatica da marina) was formed.

Naval Aviation, July 1917

On July 1917 the Navy regained control of naval aviation (that had been ceded to the Army on September 1916). Control was by the Chief of Naval Staff (Capo di Stato Maggiore) through the Inspectorate of Submarines and Aviation (Ispettorato Sommergibili e Aviazione). The Army was still furnishing, though, personnel for the stations of Porto Coraini, Ancona, Pescara, Valona (Albania), S. Maria di Leuca and for those on the Tyrrhenian Sea.

- Stazioni aeronavali:

  - Grado: eight L.3, two FBA
  - Venezia: thirteen L.3, twelve FBA and one MM
  - Porto Corsini: three FBA

- Varano, one L.1 and six L.3
- Brindisi: seven L.3 and eleven FBA
- Otranto: four L.3
- S. Maria di Leuca: three L.3
- Taranto: one L.1, three L.3 and three FBA
- Napoli: three FBA
- La Spezia: five FBA
- Varazze: three FBA
- Porto Maurizio: four FBA
- San Remo: five FBA
- R.N. Europa: eight FBA
- Valona, Albania: nine FBA

Army Aviation, August 1917

19th & 20th Balloon Sections ' self-carried ' were formed.

Army Aviation, August 1st, 1917

- Raggruppamento Squadriglie da Bombardamento (Pordenone, at Comando Supremo disposal):

  - IV Gruppo: Squadriglie 1a, 8a, 10a, 13a and 14a Caproni
  - XI Gruppo: Squadriglie 2a, 3a, 4a, 6a, 7a and 15a Caproni
  - X Gruppo (Udine): Squadriglie 70a and 82a Nieuport, 91a SPAD at S. Caterina; 114a S.P.2 at Campoformido

- Comando Aeronautica 1a Armata:

  - III Gruppo (Verona): Squadriglie 5a and 9a Caproni at Verona; 31a S.P. at Castelgomberto, 46a MF at Castenedolo, 50a MF at Villaverla, 72a SAML at Brescia and 1a Idro FBA at Desenzano.
  - IX Gruppo: Squadriglie 37a S.P.2 and S.P.3 at Ponte S.Pietro; 71a Nieuport at Villaverla, 73a SAML and 75a Nieuport at Verona and 74a MF and S.P. at Trento

- Comando Aeronautica 2a Armata:

  - II Gruppo (Udine): Squadriglie 21a, 22a, 33a, 35a and 40a S.P., 132a Pomilio at Campoformido; 27a S.P. at Chiasellis

- VI Gruppo (Oleis): Squadriglie 24a S.P., 29a MF, 113a SAML and III/83a Nieuport at Cavazzo Carnico; 41a S.P. and 45a MF at Oleis; 76a and 78a Nieuport – SPAD, 81a at Borgnano

- Comando Aeronautica 3a Armata:

  - I Gruppo (S. Maria la Longa): Squadriglie 23a S.P. and 24a Nieuport at S. Maria la Longa; 25a Voisin at Pozzuolo; 77a Nieuport – SPAD and 80a Nieuport at Aiello; 112a SAML at Lavariano, 131a Pomilio at Chiasellis and 2a Idro FBA at Grado
  - V Gruppo (Chiasottis): Squadriglie 28a S.P. at S. M. la Longa, 38a S.P. at Risano, 39a S.P. at Sammardenchia, 42a Caudron at Medeuzza, 43a Caudron at Bolzano and 44a Caudron at Gonars

- Comando Aeronautica 4a Armata:

  - XII Gruppo (Belluno): Squadriglie 48a Caudron and II/83a Nieuport at Belluno, I/113a SAML at Villaverla

- Comando Aeronautica 6a Armata:

  - VII Gruppo: Squadriglie 26a S.P. at Casoni, 32a Farman at S. Pietro in Gu, 49a Caudron at Nove and 79a Nieuport at Istrana

- VIII Gruppo (Valona, Albania): Squadriglie 11a Caproni, 34a Farman and Sezione Nieuport

- Squadriglie 47a Farman and I/83a Nieuport in Macedonia, Greece

Naval Aviation, August 15th, 1917

- Grado: ten L.3, one FBA and two M.5
- Venezia: twenty L.3, nine FBA, one M.5 and four Sopwith
- Porto Corsini: four FBA
- Varano: one L.2 and eight L.3
- Brindisi: eight L.3, twelve FBA and four Sopwith
- Otranto: five L.3
- S.M. di Leuca: four L.3
- Taranto (school): six L.1, one L.2 and four FBA

- R.N. Europa: seven FBA
- Valona, Albania: fourteen FBA

In the summer of 1917 the Navy formed the Direction of Aviation Services of Southern Italy (Direzione del servizi di aeronautica dell'Italia Meridionale). The naval traffic defence organisation, that time, comprised of stations at Palermo with two seaplanes, Milazzo with six, Napoli with two, Piombino with two, Campiglia Marittima with two Caproni, La Spezia with six, Sestri Ponente with one, Varazze with three, Porto Maurizio with six and San Remo with four.

Army Aviation, September 1917

Comando d'Aeronautica instituted a new numbering of the Squadriglie, already existing and being formed, connected with the type of plane flown by them on September 17th, 1917:

- 1a to 20a Caproni
- 21a to 40a S.P.3
- 41a to 60a SIA7B1
- 61a to 69a S.P.4
- 70a to 85a Nieuport and HD
- 86a to 100a SVA and SPAD
- 101a to 130a SAML and ' Difesa '
- 131a to 150a P
- 151a to 160a SIA7b2
- 161a to 170a SIA 9b
- 171a to 180a P500
- 181a to 189a Caproni triplanes
- 241a and further for Navy seaplanes

So, 73a and 74a SAML ' Difesa ' became 121a and 122a.
The system above was not used fully since, for example, the P.500 did not materialise, only one SIA 9b Squadriglie (161a) was formed and only two Caproni triplanes (181a and 182a).

VII Balloon Sections Group and three gas column detached sections were formed.

Army Aviation, October 1st, 1917

- Raggruppamento Squadr. da Bombardamento (Pordenone, at Comando Supremo disposal):

    - IV Gruppo (La Comina): Squadriglie 1a, 8a, 13a at Comina; 10a and 14a at Campoformido
    - XI Gruppo (Aviano): Squadriglie 2a, 3a, 4a, 6a, 7a at Aviano and 15a at Campoformido
    - X Gruppo (Udine): Squadriglie 70a and 82a Nieuport, 91a SPAD at S. Caterina; 78a Nieuport at Istrana and 132a Pomilio at Campoformido

- Comando Aeronautica 1a Armata:

    - III Gruppo (Verona): Squadriglie 5a and 9a Caproni at Campoformido; 31a S.P. at Castelgomberto, 50a MF at Villaverla, 120a SAML at Castenedolo, 1a Idro FBA at Desenzano and 3a Idro FBA at Pilzone.
    - IX Gruppo (Villaverla): Squadriglie 37a S.P.2 and S.P.3 at Castenendolo; 71a Nieuport – SPAD at Villaverla, 75a Nieuport – SPAD and 121a SAML at Verona and 122a SAML – S.P. at Trento

- Truppe degli Altipiani:

    - VII Gruppo (Nove di Bassano): Squadriglie 26a S.P.3 and 62a S.P.4 at Casoni, 32a MF at S. Pietro in Gu, 33a S.P.3 and II/115a SAML at Nove and 79a Nieuport at Istrana.

- Comando Aeronautica 2a Armata:

    - II Gruppo (Udine): Squadriglie 21a, 22a, 40a S.P., 114a SAML and 133a P at Campoformido (27a S.P. at Chiasellis at the disposition of VI Gr.)
    - VI Gruppo (Oleis): Squadriglie 24a S.P., 113a SAML and III/83a Nieuport at Cavazzo Carnico; 36a S.P. and 45a Farman (being disbanded) at Oleis; 76a Nieuport – HD – SPAD and 81a SPAD at Borgnano.

- Comando Aeronautica 3a Armata:

    - I Gruppo (S. Maria la Longa): Squadriglie 23a S.P. at S. Maria la Longa; 25a Voisin at Pozzuolo; 77a Nieuport – SPAD and 80a Nieuport at Aiello; 112a SAML and 131a Pomilio at Lavariano and 2a Idro FBA at Grado.
    - V Gruppo (Chiasottis): Squadriglie 28a S.P. at S. M. la Longa, 38a S.P. at Risano, 39a S.P. at Sammardenchia, 42a and 43a Caudron at Medeuzza and 44a Caudron at Gonars.

- Comando Aeronautica 4a Armata:

    - XII Gruppo (Belluno): Squadriglie 35a S.P.3 at S. Giustina, 48a Caudron and II/83a Nieuport at Belluno, I/115a SAML at Villaverla

- VIII Gruppo (Valona, Albania): Squadriglie 11a Caproni (Tahyraga), 34a MF and Sezione Nieuport (Tahyraga)

- Squadriglie 47a Farman and I/83a Nieuport in Thessaloniki, Macedonia, Greece

Army Aviation, October 1917

On October 19th, 1917 Comando Supremo issued a new TOE for – artillery spotting and reconnaissance - Squadriglie assigned to armies: each army was to have two Squadriglie per l'artiglieria d'armata with 9 pilots, 18 observers and 12 planes and the
' biggest possible ' number of squadriglie da Ricognizione with 12 planes each.

Squadriglie Caccia were united under X Gruppo on October 25th, 1917 at the disposition of Comando Supremo (70a, 82a and 91a Squadriglie), in the Cavazzo sottogruppo (76a, 78a and 81a Squadriglie) and the Aiello sottogruppo (77a, 80a and 84a Squadriglie).

On October 25th, 1917 a new TOE for Squadriglie di osservazione per l'artiglieria was issued: 9 planes with 9 pilots and 18 observer (one of these Squadriglie for each Army Corps) and 12 planes with 12 observers for each squadrigla di ricognizione d'armata.

All the above plans were thrown in disarray with the Italian retreat in the Caporetto front.

Balloon Service: 6 groups (of 20 sections), 1 independent balloon gas column & 3 detached sections, Venice Fortified Area Balloon Service (1 gruppo – three fortress balloon sections -), 1 special balloon group (obstructions) with 3 sections.

Army Aviation, November 1917

25a bis Floating Balloon Section (sezione aerostatica natante), 2nd & 3rd Special Balloon Sections
(sezione aerostatica speciale), I Special Balloon Sections Group were formed.

The Commissariat General of Aviation (Commisariato Generale d'Aeronautica) was created on November 1st, 1917 as part of the Ministry for Arms and Munitions (Ministero per le Armi e Munizioni) in order to co-ordinate and supervise industrial mobilization and the production of planes and motors.

On November 8th, 1917 Ufficio Servizi Aeronautici disbanded 2nd and 6th Armies' Comandi d'Aeronautica and reconstituted 4th Army Comando Aeronautica (with 2nd Army Comando Aeronautica units and personnel) and formed Comando Aeronautica per le Truppe degli Altipiani. At the same time, two new Gruppi were formed (XIII and XIV), three Squadriglie da Ricognizione were disbanded (25a, 44a and 50a), while another four (21a, 24a, 40a and 62a) moved to places not considered a war zone in order to re-equip. The order of battle, after these changes, was the following:

- 1a Armata (Verona): III and IX Gruppo
- Truppe degli Altipiani (Bassano): VII Gruppo
- 3a Armata: I, V and XIII Gruppo
- 4a Armata (Castelfranco): II, VI and XII Gruppo
- Raggruppamento Squadriglie, Comando Supremo (S. Pelagio): IV, XII and XIV Gruppo
- Comando Supremo: X Gruppo

On November 20th, 1917 there were:

- 59 squadriglie and 2 sezioni with 378 planes (59 Caproni, 9 Farman, 5 Caudron, 59 SAML 200, 1 S.P.2, 55 S.P.3, 19 S.P.4, 28 Pomilio, 6 SIA 7b, 31 Nieuport XI, 36 SPAD 140, 34 HD and 36 various types)
- 457 pilots (258 officers and 239 NCOs and privates), 284 officer observers, 152 machine-gunners
- Naval Aviation had 119 pilots (and 79 Army Aviation pilots attached).

Army Aviation, November 20th, 1917

- Aeronautica della 1a Armata (Verona):

    - III Gruppo (Verona): 37a at Brescia; 72a, 120a 1a sez./ 134a at Castenedolo and 121a at Verona.
    - IX Gruppo (Villaverla): 61a, 71a, 2a sez. / 134a at Villaverla and 31a at Castelgomberto.

- Aeronautica Truppe degli Altipiani (Bassano):

    - VII Gruppo (Nove): 33a, 2a sez. / 139a and 115a at Nova; 26a and 32a at S. Pietro in Gu and 79a at Nove and Padova.

- Aeronautica della 4a Armata (Castelfranco):

    - II Gruppo (Casoni): 113a, 114a, 132a and 133a at Casoni.
    - XII Gruppo: 27a, 48a and 35a at castel di Godego; 22a and 36a at Istrana.
    - VI Gruppo: 76a, 78a and 81a at Istrana

- Aeronautica della 3a Armata:

    - I Gruppo: 117a, 131a and 112a at Padova
    - V Gruppo: 23a and 28a at Marcon; 38a and 39a at Ca' Tessera
    - XIII Gruppo: 77a, 80a, 84a and 2a sez. / 83a at Marcon

- Comando Supremo:

- X Gruppo: 91a at Padova; 70a and 82a at Istrana.

- Raggruppamento Squadriglie da bombardamento:

  - XI Gruppo: 4a, 5a and 6a at Padova
  - IV Gruppo: 1a, 8a, 9a and 13a at S. Pelagio
  - XIV Gruppo: 2a, 3, 7a, 10a, 14a and 15a at Ghedi

- Squadriglie being re-equiped:

  - 24a at Ponte S. Pietro (passing to V Gruppo)
  - 118a Pomilio at Taliedo (passing to V Gruppo)
  - 62a at Taliedo
  - 21a and 40a at Ponte S. Pietro (re-equipping with SIA 7b)
  - 112a (at Ponte S. Pietro ?) re-equipping with PE

Flying Training Centres (Centri Formazioni Squadriglie) moved from Arcade and Ghedi to Busto Arsizio and Riva di Chieri and from S. Pelagio to Ponte San Pietro.

The Fighter Flights Inspectorate (Ispettorato Squadriglie da Caccia) was formed on November 22nd, 1917.

Documents show a number of units being disbanded in December 1917 (not all, though were actually disbanded, while all were still in a state of mobilisation):

- Gruppi I, VI, IX, XII, XIV and XVII
- Squadriglie 7a, 9a and 14a Caproni
- Squadriglia 25a Voisin
- Squadriglie 27a, 28a, 36a, 37a, 40a, 48a, 132a, 133a, 134a and 136a Pomilio
- Squadriglie 29a, 30a, 33a and 35a S.P.
- Squadriglie 34a, 45a, 46a, 47a, 49a and 50a Farman
- Squdriglie 41a, 42a, 43a and 44a Caudron
- Squadriglie 62a and 63a S.P.4
- Squadriglia 74a Balilla
- Squadriglia 76a HD

ITALIAN MILITARY AVIATION IN WORLD WAR I 1914-1918

Army Aviation, December 1917

28th Fortress Balloon Section, 2nd Naval Balloon Section and 20th Floating Balloon Section were formed.

Naval Aviation, end of December 1917

- 34 seaplanes at Venezia
- 7 at Porto Corsini
- 4 at Ancona
- 11 at Varano
- 22 at Brindisi
- 6 at Otranto
- 4 at S. Maria di Leuca
- 24 at Valona, Albania
- 8 on R.N. Europa
- 103 at various stations (San Remo, Porto Maurizio, Varazze, Rapallo, La Spezia, Campiglia, Piombino, Civitavecchia, Ponza, Napoli, Sapri, Milazzo, Catania, Syracusa and Palermo) for maritime traffic defence.

During 1917 naval aviation planned to form three bomb groups (these plans did not materialise due to the retreat on the Isonzo front, but the bomb groups with the Caproni bombers came into fruition during 1918):

- 1o gruppo (Venezia-Ferrara): 80 Caproni Ca.3 bombers, 1 large and 3 medium airships
- 2o gruppo (Chieti-Foggia): 80 Caproni Ca.3 bombers, 1 large and 2 medium airships
- 3o gruppo (Brindisi-Valona): 80 Caproni Ca.3 bombers, 1 large and 2 medium airships

Balloon units, 1917

Italy: 6 groups (I – IV, VI & VII), 18 sections ' self carried ' (1a – 7a, 9a, 11a – 20a), 1 fortress group and 4 fortress sections (25a – 28a) in Venezia, I Aerial Obstructions Group with 3 sections (1a, 2a & 3a) in Venezia, 2 floating sections (20a bis & 25a bis) in Venezia, 2 navy sections (1a in Taranto & 2a in Brindisi)
Albania: 10th Section ' self-carried '

Macedonia, Greece: 8th Section ' self carried '

1918

In the last year of the war, Italian Military Aviation reached its zenith, with Army Aviation alone peaking at 64 squadriglie and 6 sezioni. Army aircraft strength reached 820 with 940 pilots. In addition there were observers and machine-gunners.

Army Aviation, January 1st, 1918

- I Gruppo: 112a, 117a and 131a
- II Gruppo: 113a, 114a, 132a and 133a
- III Gruppo: 61a, 75a and 134a
- IV Gruppo: 1a, 8a, 13a and 15a
- V Gruppo: 23a, 28a, 38a, 39a and 118a
- VI Gruppo: 76a, 78a and 81a
- VII Gruppo: 26a, 32a and 33a
- VIII Gruppo: 11a, 85a and 116a
- IX Gruppo: 37a, 72a, 120a and 135a
- X Gruppo: 70a, 82a and 91a
- XI Gruppo: 4a, 5a and 6a
- XII Gruppo: 22a, 27a, 35a, 36a and 48a
- XIII Gruppo: 77a, 80a and 83a
- XIV Gruppo: 2a, 3a, 7a, 9a, 10a and 14a
- XV Gruppo: 79a, 115a and 139a
- XVI Gruppo: 31a, 71a and 121a
- XVIII Gruppo: 3a, 14a and 15a
- Gruppo Settentrionale Difesa: 112a and Sezioni Piacenza, Ponte S. Pietro, Taliedo, Cameri, Malpensa and Mirafiori
- Gruppo Centrale Difesa: Sezioni Firenze, Bologna, Ravenna, Rimini, Cairo Montenotte and Novi Ligure
- Gruppo Meridionale Difesa: 107a, 101a and Sezioni Ancona, Jesi and Terni
- Independent Squadriglie: 73a in Macedonia – Greece, 111a in Macedonia – Greece, 106a in Libya, 12a in Libya and Sezione Difesa Tripoli

In January a new numbering of balloon units was ordered:

V Group became XXI
I Special Group became XLI
25th – 28th Fortress Sections became 51st – 54th
20a bis & 25a bis Floating Sections became 55a & 60a respectively
The two navy sections became 71a & 72a
The three special sections became 91a, 92a & 93a

73rd Navy Balloon Section, 94th Special Balloon Section & 31st ' self carried ' Section were formed.

Army Aviation, February 1918

4th Army Comando Aeronautica was reformed on February 1st, 1918 (with headquarters at Cittadella).

It was decided, on February 22nd, 1918 to form six Sezioni SVA with SVA planes with narrow wings, each of six pilots and six planes. The three, already existing, Sezioni were assigned thus: 1a Sezione SVA to 1st Army at Sovizzo, 2a Sezione SVA to Truppe degli Altipiani at Nove and 3a Sezione SVA to the 4th Army at Isola di Carturo. Each Sezione SVA was equivalent to a Squadriglia. SVA planes with wide wings formed two Squadriglie (the first being 87a).

1st Balloonists Group (raggruppamento aerostieri) was formed.

Army Aviation, March 1st, 1918

- Comando d'Aeronautica del Comando Supremo:

    - IV Gruppo (San Pelagio): 1a, 5a, 8a and 13a at San Pelagio
    - XI Gruppo (Verona): 4a and 6a at Verona, 181a at Ghedi
    - XIV Gruppo (Padova): 2a, 7a, 9a, 10a and 16a at Padova
    - X Gruppo (Istrana): 70a and 82a at Istrana, 87a at Ghedi, 91a at Quinto and 5a.
    - Sezione Difesa Padova

- Comando d'Aeronautica 1a Armata:

- III Gruppo (Verona): 61, 75a, 134a and 1a Sez. Farman at Verona
- IX Gruppo (Castenedolo): 37a, 62a, 72a, 120a and Sez. Difesa at Castenedolo, 113a at Medole
- XVI Gruppo (Sovizzo): 31a, 71a, 121a, 135a and 1a Sez. SVA at Sovizzo

- Comando Aeronautica Truppe degli Altipiani:

  - VII Gruppo (Nove di Bassano): 26a, 32a, 33a, 3a sez. / 24a at Nove di Bassano
  - XV Gruppo (S. Pietro in Gu): 78a and 79a at Nove, 115a and 139a at S. Pietro in Gu and 2a Sez. SVA at Nove

- Comando d'Aeronautica 3a Armata:

  - I Gruppo (Fossalunga): 112a, 117a and 131a at Fossalunga
  - V Gruppo (Carpenedo): 23a, 28a, 118a and 1a sez. / 24a at Marcon; 38a and 39a at Ca' Tessera
  - XIII Gruppo (Marcon): 77a and 80a at Marcon

- Comando d'Aeronautica 4a Armata:

  - II Gruppo (Casoni): 114a, 132a and 113a at Casoni
  - VI Gruppo (Rossano): 76a and 81a at Isola di Carturo
  - XII Gruppo (Cittadella): 22a, 35a, 36a and 2a sez. / 24a at Casoni; 27a and 48a at Castel di Godego

- VIII Gruppo (Valona, Albania; assigned to XVI Army Corps): 11a at Tahyraga, 85a at Piskupi and 116a at Valona

- Squadriglie 35a and 111a in Thessaloniki, Greece (assigned to 35th Division)

- XVIII Gruppo (France): 3a, 14a and 15a

- Squadriglie 12a, 106a and Sez. Difesa in Tripoli, Libya; 104a in Benghazi, Libya.

Army Aviation, March 1918

On March 1st, 1918 Ufficio Servizi Aeronautica was replaced by Comando Superiore di Aeronautica.

On March 17th, 1918 Squadriglie Aeroplani were distributed anew to the major formations (armies etc.). 2nd Army Comando d'Aeronautica was reformed, 7th Army's was formed and 6th Army's became Ufficio di Aeronautica.

Army Aviation, Middle of March, 1918

- Comando Aeronautica 1a Armata:

    - III Gruppo Ricognizione d'Armata e Caccia: 134a Pomilio (Verona), 135a Pomilio (Sovizzo), 75a Nieuport (Verona), 71a SPAD (Sovizzo), 1a Sezione SVA (Verona) and Sezione Farman (attached to 75a Nieuport, Verona)
    - XVI Gruppo Squadriglie di Corpo d'Armata (all Squadriglie at Sovizzo): 31a S.P.3 61a S.P.4, 121a SAML

- Comando Aeronautica 2a Armata:

    - XV Gruppo Ricognizione d'Armata e Caccia (all Squadriglie at S. Luca): 78a Hanriot , 79a Nieuport, 115a SAML and 139a Pomilio
    - XIX Gruppo Squadriglie di Corpo d'Armata (all Squadriglie at Istrana): 114a SAML, 118a SAML and 3a Sez. / 24a

- Comando Aeronautica 3a Armata:

    - I Gruppo Ricognizione d'Armata (all Squadriglie at Fossalunga): 117a SAML and 131a Pomilio
    - V Gruppo Squadriglie di Corpo d'Armata: 28a SIA (Marcon), 38a SIA (Ca' Tessera), 29a S.P.3 (Ca' Tessera), 62a S.P.4 (Marcon) and 1a Sez. / 24a (Marcon)
    - XIII Gruppo Caccia (all Squadriglie at Marcon): 77a SPAD and 80a Hanriot

- Comando Aeronautica 4a Armata:

- II Gruppo Ricognizione d'Armata (all Squadriglie at Isola di Carturo): 132a Pomilio, 133a Pomilio and 3a Sez. SVA
- VI Gruppo Caccia (all Squadriglie at Casoni): 76a Hanriot and 81a Nieuport
- XII Gruppo Squadriglie di Corpo d'Armata: 22a SIA (Casoni), 27a SIA (Castel di Godego), 35a SIA (Casoni), 36a SIA (Casoni), 48a Caudron G.4 (Castel di Godego) and 2a Sez. / 24a (Casoni)

- Ufficio Aeronautica 6a Armata:

  - VII Gruppo Sq. di Corpo d'Armata e Caccia (all Squadriglie at S. Pietro in Gu): 26a S.P.3, 32a SIA, 33a S.P.3 and 1a Sez. / 83a

- Aeronautica 7a Armata:

  - IX Gruppo Ricognizione d'Armata e Caccia (all Squadriglie at Castenedolo): 72a Hanriot, 2a Sez. / 83a, 120a SAML, 2a Sez. SVA and Sez. Farman (attached to 72a Hanriot)
  - XX Gruppo Squadriglie di Corpo d'Armata (all Squadriglie at Castenedolo): 37a S.P.3 and 40a SIA

- Comando Supremo:

  - Raggruppamento Squadriglie da Bombardamento:

    - IV Gruppo (all Squadriglie at San Pelagio): 1a Caproni, 5a Caproni, 8a Caproni and 13a Caproni

    - XI Gruppo: 4a Caproni (Verona), 6a Caproni (Verona) and 181a Ca.4 (Ghedi)

    - XIV Gruppo (all Squadriglie at Padova): 2a Caproni, 7a Caproni, 9a Caproni, 10a Caproni and 16a Caproni

    - X Gruppo Caccia: 70a Hanriot (Istrana), 82a Hanriot (Istrana), 91a SPAD (Quinto) and 87a SVA (Ghedi)

The new March 1918 TOEs (March 17th), that were never applied fully but show the optimism of the Italian High Command - provided:

- 36 planes and pilots in six Sezioni for the Squadriglie Caccia
- 14 planes for Squadriglie di Corpo d'Armata to be equipped with new SIA 7b2s (Squadriglie being equipped with this new reconnaissance plane were: 22a, 23a, 26a, 27a, 28a, 31, 32a, 33a, 35a, 36a, 37a, 38a, 39a, 48a, 61a, 62a, 114a, 118a, 121a and – abroad – 111a and 116a)
- 12 planes, Pomilio E or F, for Squadriglie da Ricognizione d'Armata (Squadriglie being equipped with Pomilio E or F: 113a, 117a and 120a)
- 8 – or more – Caproni 600 or Caproni triplanes for Squadriglie da Bombardamento

The inability to actually apply the new TOEs was due to SIA 7b's failure, Ca. 600's series of problems – which forced Ca. 450 to remain in production, in the end of 1918 the number of Ca.450s in front-line service was the same as in 1916 -. Squadriglie da Caccia did not have 36 planes at the end of the war but 18.

Army Aviation, April 1918

On April 10th, 1918 Entente forces had the following numbers of planes on the Italian front (6th Wing, Royal Naval Air Service planes - at Otranto - and other Entente forces not on the Italian front – northern Italy – not included):

	Fighter	Bombers	Reconnaissance
Italy	232	66	205
France	-	-	20
Great Britain	54	-	26
TOTALS	286	66	251

ITALIAN MILITARY AVIATION IN WORLD WAR I 1914-1918

Army Aviation, May 1918

On May 25th, 1918 Comando d'Aeronautica del Comando Supremo was replaced by Comando Aeronautica a Disposizione.

From March to May, VIII & IX Groups, six ' self carried ' sections (32a – 37a), one special section (95th), Balloon Material Central Depot (deposito centrale materiale aerostatico), five Army balloon supply sections (Sezione rifornimenti aerostatici d'armata) & 2nd Independent Gas Column were formed.

Army Aviation, June 1918

On June 12th, 1918, 8th Army's Comando Aeronautica was formed and 2nd Army's was disbanded.

In the beginning of June 1918 the March 1918 plan for a re-equipment air units equipped with SAMLs with Pomilios was changed: Squadriglia 121a (1a Armata), 39a (3a Armata) and 118a (8a Armata) retained their SAML before re-equipping with Pomilios, while only 23a, 26a, 48a 61a, 62a and 114a re-equipped with it. Units that were to replace their S.P.3s, S.P.4s and Caudron G.4s retained them.

On June 5th, 1918 the Massa di Manovra Squadriglie da Caccia was formed (Squadriglie 70a, 72a, 75a, 76a, 79a, 80a, 82a, 91a).

In the middle of June, 1918 Army Aviation had: 65 squadriglie and 9 sezioni with 647 planes (of which three quarters in use), 770 pilots, 474 observers, 176 machine-gunners.

Army Aviation, Middle of June, 1918

- Comando dell'Aeronautica a Disposizione (Padova):

    - IV Gruppo (all Squadriglie at S. Pelagio): 1a (six Ca.450), 5a (four Ca.450), 8a (five Ca.450) and 13a (three Ca.450), 87a (seventeen SVA)
    - XIV Gruppo (all Squadriglie at Padova): 2a (three Ca.450), 7a (five Ca.450), 9a (four Ca.450), 10a (four Ca.450)

- XI Gruppo: 4a (at Ca' degli Oppi with seven Ca.450), 6a (at Ca' degli Oppi with five Ca.450), 181a (at Ghedi with eight Ca. Triplano)
- X Gruppo: 70a (at Gazzo with eighteen HD), 82a (at Gazzo with twenty one HD), 91a (at Quinto di Treviso with seventeen SPAD XIII)

- Comando dell'Aeronautica della 1a Armata:

  - III Gruppo: 61a (at Ganfardine with eight S.P.4), 75a (at Busiago with fifteen Nieuport 27 and HD), 134a (at Ganfardine with fourteen Pomilio), 1a S. SVA (with six SVA)
  - XVI Gruppo (all Squadriglie at Castelgomberto): 31a (six S.P.3 and SIA), 71a (thirteen SPAD and HD), 121a (seven SAML), 135a (ten Pomilio PE)

- Comando dell'Aeronautica della 8a Armata:

  - XV Gruppo (all Squadriglie at San Luca): 78a (twenty HD), 79a (sixteen Nieuport 27 and HD), 115a (seven SAML and PE), 139a (eight Pomilio PE), 4a Sez. SVA (six SVA)
  - XIX Gruppo (all Squadriglie at Istrana): 23a (five S.P.3), 114a (six SAML), 118a (seven SAML), III / 24a

- Comando dell'Aeronautica della 3a Armata:

  - I Gruppo: 117a (at Fossalunga with seven Pomilio PE), 5a Sez. SVA (at Fossalunga with seven SVA), 28a (at Marcon with four SIA7b), 38a (at Malcontenta with six SIA7b), 39a (at Malcontenta with eleven SAML), 62a (at Marcon with four S.P.4 and PE), 131a (at Marcon with ten Pomilio PE), I / 24a
  - XIII Gruppo (all Squadriglie at Marcon): 77a (sixteen SPAD and HD), 80a (fifteen HD)

- Comando dell'Aeronautica della 4a Armata:

  - II Gruppo (all Squadriglie at Isola di Carturo): 132a (eleven Pomilio PE), 133a (ten Pomilio PE), 3a Sez. SVA (eight SVA)
  - VI Gruppo (all Squadriglie at Casoni): 76a (seventeen HD), 81a (twenty HD and Nieuport 27)

- XII Gruppo: 22a (at Casoni with four SIA7b), 27a (at Castel di Godego with one SIA7b), 35a (at Castel di Godego with five SIA7b), 36a (at Casoni with four SIA7b), 48a (at Castel di Godego with three Caudron G.4), II / 24a (at Casoni with three SIA7b)

- Comando dell'Aeronautica della 6a Armata:

    - VII Gruppo: 26a (at S. Pietro in Gu with twelve S.P.3 and SIA), 32a (at S. Pietro in Gu with nine SIA7b), 33a (at S. Pietro in Gu with five S.P.3), 83a (at Poianella with twenty HD and Nieuport 27), 2a Sez. SVA (at Poianella with six SVA)

- Comando dell'Aeronautica della 7a Armata:

    - IX Gruppo: 72a (at Busiago with eleven HD), 74a (at Castenedolo with seventeen Nieuport 27 and HD), 112a (at Castenedolo with eleven Pomilio PE), 120a (at Castenedolo with three SAML and PE), 136a (at Castenedolo with ten Pomilio PE), 6a Sez. SVA (at Castenedolo with seven SVA)
    - XX Gruppo: 37a (at ponte S. Marco with seven S.P.3 and SIA), 40a (at Pian Camuno with two SIA7b), 113a (at Medole with three Pomilio PE)

- VIII Gruppo (for XVI Army Corps in Albania): 11a (at Tahyraga with four Ca.450), 85a (at Piskupi with sixteen Nieuport 17 and HD), 116a (at Valona with nine SAML)

- XXI Gruppo (for 35th Division in Thessaloniki, Greece): 73a (at Thessaloniki with eleven Nieuport and SPAD), 111a (at Kremjan with twelve SAML)

- XVIII Gruppo (in France): 3a (at Ochey with sixteen Ca.450), 15a (at Ochey with four Ca.450)

On June 28th a new T.O.E. for Squadriglie da Ricognizione was established with twelve planes, fourteen pilots and fourteen observers (officer pilots were not to exceed five in each Squadriglia). Two or three Pomilio Squadriglie (of about twelve planes each) and one SAML or S.P.3 Squadriglia was assigned to each Army.

In June the following Squadriglie were re-equipped with Pomilio:

- 23a, 32a and 33a (replacing S.P.3)
- 61a and 62a (replacing S.P.4)
- 113a, 114a, 117a and 120a (replacing SAML)
- 48a (replacing Caudron G.4)

Squadriglie 26a, 31a and 37a (equipped with S.P.3) were assigned SIA 7b to be re-equipped with.

Army Aviation, July 1918

In the beginning of July the following Squadriglie were disbanded: 24a, 35a, 37a, 40a, 62a, 117a, 132a, 133a, 135a and 139a.

Army Aviation, after July 7th, 1918

- Comando d'Aeronautica a disposizione:

    - IV Gruppo: 1a, 5a, 8a and 13a
    - XI Gruppo: 4a, 6a and 87a
    - XIV Gruppo: 2a, 7a, 9a and 10a
    - X Gruppo: 70a, 82a and 91a

- Comando d'Aeronautica 1a Armata:

    - III Gruppo: 61a P (Ganfardine), 75a Nieuport (Ganfardine), 134a P (Ganfardine), 1a Sez. SVA (Ganfardine) and Sez. S.P.3 Difesa Verona
    - XVI Gruppo (Castelgomberto with all Squadriglie at Castelgomberto): 31a P, 71a SPAD – HD and 121a SAML

- Comando d'Aeronautica 3a Armata:

    - I Gruppo (at Fossalunga with all Squadriglie at Fossalunga): 131a P and 5a Sez. SVA
    - V Gruppo (Malcontenta): 28a P / S.P.3 (Marcon), 38a P (Malcontenta) and 39a SAML (Malcontenta)

- XIII Gruppo (at Marcon with all Squadriglie at Marcon): 77a SPAD and 80a HD

- Comando d'Aeronautica 2a Armata:

  - II Gruppo (at Castel di Godego with all Squadriglie at Castel di Godego): 27a P and 48a P
  - VI Gruppo (at Casoni): 76a HD (Casoni), 81a Ni / HD (Casoni) and 3a Sez. SVA
  - XII Gruppo (at Casoni with all Squadriglie at Casoni): 22a P and 36a P

- Comando d'Aeronautica 7a and 9a Armata:

  - XXIV Gruppo (Castenedolo): 72a HD (Castenedolo), 74a HD (Castenedolo) and Sez. 74a HD (Cividate Camuno)
  - IX Gruppo (Castenedolo): 112a P (Castenedolo), 120a P (Medole) and 6a Sez. SVA (Castenedolo)
  - XX Gruppo (Brescia): 113a SAML (Cividate Camuno) and 136a P (Ponte San Marco)

- Comando d'Aeronautica 8a Armata:

  - XXIII Gruppo (at San Luca with all Squadriglie at San Luca): 78a HD and 79a Nieuport
  - XV Gruppo (Paese): 115a SAML (San Luca) and 4a Sez. SVA (San Luca)
  - XIX Gruppo (Falze): 23a P (Istrana), 114a P (Istrana) and 118a P (Istrana)

- Ufficio d'Aeronautica 6a Armata:

  - VII Gruppo (S. Pietro in Gu): 26a P (S. Pietro in Gu), 32a P (S. Pietro in Gu), 33a P (S. Pietro in Gu), 83a Ni / HD (Pojanella) and 2a Sez. SVA (Pojanella)
  - XXII Gruppo Caproni (Ghedi with all Squadriglie at Ghedi): 181a and 182a

- VIII Gruppo (in Albania for XVI Army Corps): 11a, 85a and 116a

- XXI Gruppo (in Macedonia, Greece for 35th Division): 73a and 111a

- XVIII Gruppo (in France with all Squadriglie at Villeneuve): 3a, 14a and 15a

- 12a and 106a Squadriglie in Libya

Army Aviation, October 1918

On October 23rd, 1918 the Massa da Caccia was reformed with Squadriglie 91a, 71a and 72a at Quinto, 70a and 82a at Gazzo and reinforced with British fighters. At the same time the Massa da Bombardamento (nine Squadriglie) was formed with Gruppo IV (at San Pelagio), XI (at Padova) and XIV (at Arqua Petrarca) as were XXII Gruppo di bombardamento SVA (at Busiago), Regia Marina Gruppo Triplani, Squadriglie 181a and 182a, Stormo SIA 9b of the Squadriglia ' San Marco ', 161a Squadriglia SIA 9b and two Ca.600 Squadriglie (203a and 204a).

Strategic reconnaissance was assigned to 87a Squadriglia ' Serenissima ' under the direct command of Comando and a Sezione Speciale SVA was formed named Aviazione per le Divisioni di Cavalleria.

Finally Comando d'Aeronautica 10a Armata (28a Squadriglia PE – ex-3rd Army – and British units) and Comando Aeronautica 12a Armata (48a Squadriglia PE – ex-4th Army and French units) were formed.

On October 24th, 1918 flights and sections at the frontline were: 30 reconnaissance flights and 9 sections, 15 bomb flights, 15 fighter flights and 4 sections, 36 balloon sections and 7 dirigibles.

On the same date the Ballonists Battalion became Balloonists Command (Comando Aerostieri) and the Airships-Balloons Depot (deposito d'aeronautica – dirigibilisti- aerostieri) became Balloons & Airships Supply Centre (Centro Rifornimento Aerostieri e Dirigibilisti).

The 2nd Balloonists Grouping was formed.

Army Aviation, October 30th, 1918

	Squadriglie	Sezioni	Planes	Pilots	Observers	Machine-gunners
Fighter	16	-	341	320	-	-
Servizio di C.d'A.	26	-	249	297	318	-
Strategic reconnaissance	3	5	108	91	19	-
Caproni bombers	13	-	69	167	66	105
Gruppo I	1	1	8	14	6	6
SIA 9b bombers	1	-	11	6	7	2
SVA special	2	-	22	35	-	-
Seaplanes	1	-	7	5	5	6
Squadriglia U.M.	1	-	5	5	5	-
TOTALS	64	6	820	940	426	119

From July to October, X Balloon Group, eight 'self carried' balloon sections (38a – 45a), XXV Floating Balloon Sections Group, 74th & 75th Navy Sections and 96th, 97th & 101st Special Balloon Sections were formed.

Army Aviation, November 4th, 1918 (aircraft numbers are for operational aircraft)

- Aeronautica del Comando Supremo:

    - Massa Di Caccia:

        - X Gruppo (Gazzo and all Squadriglie at Gazzo): 70a (eighteen HD) and 82a (nineteen HD)
        - XVII Gruppo (Quinto di Treviso): 91a (at Quinto di Treviso, twelve SPAD), 71a (at Quinto di Treviso, thirteen SPAD), 72a (at Quinto di Treviso, thirteen HD) and 77a (at Marcon, thirteen SPAD)

- Massa da Bombardamento:

  - IV Gruppo (San Pelagio and all Squadriglie at San Pelagio): 1a (two Ca.3), 5a (two Ca.3), 8a (three Ca.3) and 13a (one Ca.3)
  - XIV Gruppo (at Arqua Petrarca and all Squadriglie at Arqua Petrarca): 2a (one Ca.3), 7a (four Ca.3) and 10a (three Ca.3)
  - XI Gruppo (at Padova and all Squadriglie at Padova): 4a (no serviceable Ca.3) and 6a (seven Ca.5)
  - XXII Gruppo (at Busiago and all Squadriglie at Busiago): 89a (ten SVA 6) and 90a (eight SVA 5)
  - Regia Marina (Royal Italian Navy, at P.o Renato): 181a (three Ca.4) and 182a (three Ca.4)

- 1 S.A. (Venezia, with SVA, SIA and Ca.7)

- 87a Squadriglia (S. Pelagio, fourteen SVA)

- Sez. Cavalleria (S. Pelagio, seven SVA)

- Airships: F5, F6, M19, M11 and M14

- Comando Aeronautica della 3a Armata (Carpenedo):

  - V Gruppo (Carpenedo): 38a (Malcontenta, six PE) and 39a (Malcontenta, five PE)
  - XIII Gruppo (Marcon): 80a (Marcon, thirteen HD)
  - I Gruppo (Carpenedo): 131a (Marcon, seven PE) and 5a Sez. SVA (Carpenedo, six SVA)

- Sp. I (Ca' Tessera, all Squadriglie at Ca' Tessera): 9a (three Ca.3) and Mista (three planes)

- Comando Aeronautica della 8a Armata (Albaredo):

  - XV Gruppo (Paese): 115a (Fossalunga, fifteen SAML) and 56a (Fossalunga, fifteen SAML)
  - XIX Gruppo (Falze): 23a (Istrana, six PE), 114a (Istrana, ten PE) and 118a (Istrana, PE)
  - XXIII (S. Luca and all Squadriglie at S. Luca): 78a (sixteen HD) and 79a (eighteen HD)

- Comando Aeronautica della 4a Armata (Bolzanella):

    - II Gruppo (at Cast. di Godego and all Squadriglie at Cast. di Godego): 27a (eight PE) and 48a (?)
    - VI Gruppo (at Casoni and all Squadriglie at Casoni): 76a (seventeen HD) and 81a (seventeen HD)
    - XII Gruppo (at Casoni and all Squadriglie at Casoni): 22a (four PE) and 36a (eight PE)
    - 21a Squadriglia (Is. di Carturo, seven SAML)
    - 57a Squadriglia (Is. di Carturo, eight SVA)

- Comando Aeronautica della 6a Armata (Breganze):

    - VII Gruppo (S. Pietro in Gu and all Squadriglie at S. Pietro in Gu): 26a (six PE), 32a (seven PE) and 33a (six S.P.3)
    - XXIV Gruppo (Poianella): 83a (Poianella, fourteen Nieuport), 2a Sez. SVA (Poianella, two SVA) and 136a (Villaverla, no serviceable PE)

- Comando Aeronautica della 1a Armata (S. Martino Buonalbergo):

    - III Gruppo (Ganfardine): 61a (Ganfardine, four PE), 75a (Ganfardine, seventeen Nieuport), 134a (Ganfardine, two PE), 1a Sez. SVA (Ganfardine, three SVA), 1a Sez. Idro (Desenzano, three FBA) and 2a Sez. Idro (Desenzano, three FBA)
    - XVI Gruppo (Castelgomberto and all Squadriglie at Castelgomberto): 31a (seven PE), 121a (three SAML) and 134B (two PE)

- Comando Aeronautica della 7a Armata (Brescia):

    - XX Gruppo (Brescia): 74a (Ponte S. Marco, ten HD), 113a (Cividate Cam., three SAML) and 120a (Ponte S. Marco, five PE)
    - IX Gruppo (Castenedolo and all Squadriglie at Castenedolo): 112a (three PE) and 6a Sez. SVA (two SVA)

- Comando Aeronautica della 10a Armata:

    - 28a Squadriglia (Malcontenta, six PE)
    - 34 Escadrille (French, fourteen AR)
    - 139th RAF Squadron (British, ten F2B)
    - 28th RAF Squadron (British, sixteen Camel)
    - 66th RAF Squadron (British, eighteen Camel)

- Comando Aeronautica della 12a Armata:

    - 48a (Cast. di Godego, seven PE)
    - Sez. 48a (four PE)
    - 22 Escadrille (French, ten AR)
    - 254 Escadrille (French, ten AR)
    - 561 Escadrille (French, six SPAD)

- XVIII Gruppo (in Chernizey, France): 3a (fourteen Ca.3) and 14a (Ca.3)

- VIII Gruppo (in Valona, Albania): 11a (Tahyraga with Ca.3), 85a (iskupi with Nieuport) and 116a (Valona with SAML)

- XXI Gruppo (in Thessaloniki, Greece): 73a (Dudular with Nieuport) and 111a (Dudular with SAML)

- 12a Squadriglia (in Tripoli, Libya, with Ca.3)

- 106a Squadriglia (in Tripoli, Libya, with Farman)

There were 24 Gruppi – and one Regia Marina Gruppo - (84 Squadriglie) and 6 (7 ?) Sezioni at the front (1055 planes). There also were units abroad and the 20 (13 ?) Squadriglie and 6 Sezioni da Difesa with 114 planes.

XI 'self carried' Balloon Group formed in November 1918.

Naval Aviation, November 1918

Naval Aviation had 103 planes and 241 seaplanes in the Adriatic Sea front, 5 planes and 140 seaplanes for the Squadriglie di Difesa del

Traffico and 13 airships (Naval Aviation is also mentioned as having 46 Squadriglie with 638 or 650 planes).

Naval Aviation had the following resources on the Otranto Barrage during 1918:

- 5 L.3 sea-planes (from Santa Maria di Leuca)
- 9 L.3 sea-planes and on D.E. (SSA) dirigible (from Otranto)
- 14 FBA sea-planes from Valona, Albania
- 8 FBA sea-planes aboard R.N. ' Europa '
- 26 seaplanes (from Otranto)
- 18 reconnaissance sea-planes and 4 fighter sea-planes (from Varano)
- 1 dirigible and 5 fighter planes (from Grottaglie)
- 4 D.E. (SS)-type dirigibles and 5 fighter sea-planes (from S. Vito di Taranto)

On November 10th, 1918 Comando Superiore di Aeronautica became Comando Generale d'Aeronautica and Regia Aeronautica came into being in 1923.

Balloon units, 1918

Italy: two Balloonists Groupings (1st & 2nd), nine Groups (I – IV, VI – X), thirty-one ' self carried ' sections (1a, 2a, 4a – 7a, 9a, 11a – 20a, 31a – 43a & 45a), XXV Floating Group with 55th & 60th Sections in Venezia, XLI Aerial Obstructions Group with 5 sections (91st to 93rd in Venezia, 94th in Ancona & 95th in Taranto), three navy sections (71st in Taranto, 72nd in Brindis & 73rd in Siracusa).
Albania: 10th ' self carried ' Section.
Macedonia – Greece: 8th ' self carried ' Section.
Libya: XI ' self carried ' Group with 3rd & 44th.

APPENDIX

Glossary and Abbreviations

aereo: plane, aerial
aeronave (pl. aeronavi): airship
altipiani: highlands
antiaerea: anti-aircraft
aerea: aerial
aeronavale – aeronavali: aeronaval (singular and plural, i.e. naval aviation)
aeronautico / aeronautica – aeronautici: aeronautical (singular and plural, i.e. aviation)
aeroplano – aeroplani: airplane - airplanes
aerostatico: balloon
armata: Army
armi: arms (i.e. weapons)
artiglieria (art.): artillery
autocampale: a field unit on trucks
autocarreggiate: ' self-carried '(i.e. with their own means of transport)
autonoma: autonomous (i.e. independent)
avanzato: advanced
aviatore - aviatori: aviator –aviators
aviazione: aviation
battaglione - battaglioni: Battalion - Battalions
biplano - biplani: biplane – biplanes
bombardamento: bombing
caccia: fighter
Capo di Stato Maggiore: Chief of Staff
cavalleria: cavalry
centrale: central
centro: centre
colonna: column
comando – comandi : command - commands
combattimento (comb.): combat
commisariato: commissariat

corpo: corps
deposito: depot
difesa: defence
direzione: direction
dirigibile: dirigible
disposizione: at the disposition of…
divisione – divisioni: division - divisions
formazione: training
fortezza: fortress
generale: general
gruppo – gruppi (gr.): Group - Groups
idrovolante – idrovolanti (idro): seaplane – seaplanes
ispettorato: inspectorate
massa (as in Massa da Bombardamento or Massa da Caccia): literally mass (i.e. concentration of…, temporary grouping, no available English term)
materiale: material
ministero: ministry
munizioni: munitions
natante: floating
nazionale: national
offesa: offensive (i.e. attack)
ostruzione: obstruction
osservazione: observation
raggruppamento: grouping (a term denoting a unit / higher formation between a regiment and a brigade)
Regia Aeronautica: Royal (Italian) Air Force
Regia Marina: Royal (Italian) Navy
Regia Nave (R.N.): Royal Ship
ricognizione (ric.): reconnaissance
rifornimento: supply
scuola: school
servizio – servizi: service - services
sezione – sezioni (sez. / s.): Section – Sections
sommergibili: submarines
sottogruppo –sottogruppi: Sub-group – Subgroups
speciale: special
squadriglia – Squadriglie (squadr. / sq.): Flight – Flights
staccato: detached
stazione: station

stormo: (a term to denote two or more Gruppi in World War II)
superiore: higher
supremo: highest
traffico: traffic
triplano – triplani: triplane - triplanes
truppe: troops
ufficio: office
volo: flight
zona: zone

Italian airships during World War 1 list

A.1
V.1, V.2
F.4, F.5, F.6
M.1, M.2, M.3, M.4, M.6, M.7, M.8, M.9, M.11, M.13, M.14, M.15, M.16, M.17, M.18 (some were M.-type, others M.a.-type, media cubartura alta quota – medium volume high height -)
P.2 (N.2), P.4, P.5, P.7
PV.0, PV.1, PV.2, PV.3 (Piccolo Veloce – low speed -)
U.5
O.1, O.2, O.3, O.4
DE.1 to DE. 13, DE.18, DE.19, DE.24, DE.25 (Dirigibile Esploratore – reconnaissance dirigible -)
SS.5, SS.6, SS.10, SS16 (Sea Scout)

Italian Military Aviation in World War I notes

- Flights, until December 1st, 1915 when the system was dissolved, were designated by a number and the type of plane flown by the unit (i.e. 5a Voisin). Then flights assumed their role in their designations (i.e. 8a Nieuport became 1a Squadriglia Caccia).
- Aircraft used by the various Squadriglie and their numbers, where available, are in parentheses before the landing field where the Squadriglie were based.

Italian Military Aviation in World War I sources

- Chiusano, Amedeo & Saporiti, Maurizio (SME /US), Palloni, ditigibili ed aerei del Regio Esercito 1884-1923 (Balloons, dirigibles and planes of the Royal Army 1884-1923), Roma: SME/US, 1998
- Della Volpe, Nicola (SME/US), ' Difesa del territorio e protezione antiaerea (1915-1943) Storia, documenti, immagini ' (Territorial defence and anti-aircraft protection – History, documents, pictures), Roma: SME/US, 1986
- Dell'Uomo F. & Roberto di Rosa, L'Esercito Italiano verso il 2000 – I corpi disciolti (The Italian Army towards 2000 – Disbanded Corps) Volume Secondo Tomo II, SME/US, Roma: 2001
- Gentilli, R. and Varriale, P. / Ufficio Storico dello Stato Maggiore dell' Aeronautica,
- ' I reparti dell'aviazione Italiana nella Grande Guerra ' (Italian aviation units in the Great War), Roma: Ufficio Storico dello Stato Maggiore dell' Aeronautica, 1999
- Mowthorpe, Ces, Battlebags – British airships of the First World War, Stroud: Wrens Park (Sutton), 1995 / 1998

www.ingramcontent.com/pod-product-compliance
Lightning Source LLC
Chambersburg PA
CBHW080349170426
43194CB00014B/2741